Reading Comprehension

This book belongs to

Gone Fishing

Jason and José were lucky fishermen. Jason dropped his hook in deep water and caught a carp. He went on to catch three more! José kept his hook close to the shore and caught a catfish right away. By the end of the day, the boys had nine fish altogether!

Gone Fishing (continued)

Read the sentences from the story. Color the fish **red** if the sentence describes Jason. Color it *yellow* if it describes José.

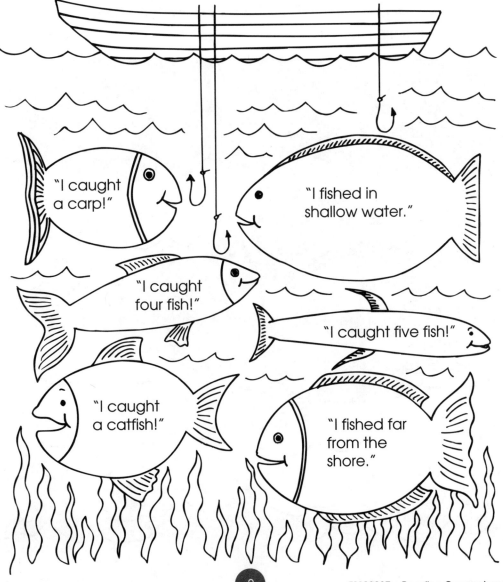

A Whale of a Tale

Have you ever wondered how a whale sleeps?
Whales float close to the top of the water. Part of their
brains stay awake so they can remember to breathe.
Every so often, they come to the surface to breathe.
What a restless night!

A Whale of a Tale (continued)

Use information from the story to write three sentences about the way a whale sleeps. Then, write three sentences about the way you sleep.

Hawaii

Hawaii was the last state to become part of the United States. It is the 50th state. Hawaii is made up of eight large islands and many small islands. The islands are mountains that were made long ago under the ocean. Some mountains in Hawaii still shoot out steam and melted rock. Sugar cane and pineapples grow in Hawaii. People in Hawaii enjoy warm weather and colorful flowers.

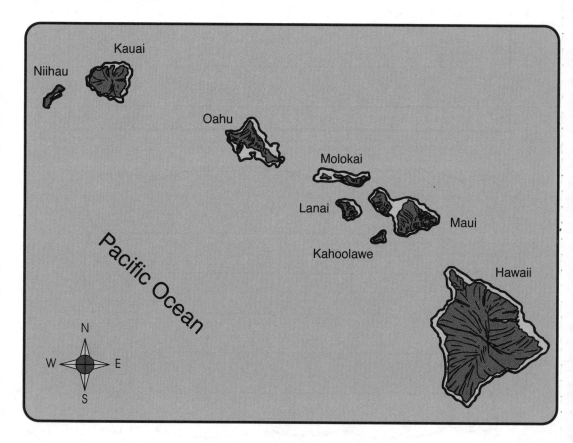

Hawaii (continued)

Use facts from the story to fill in the crossword puzzle. The Word Box will help you

Word Box

Hawaii
mountains
islands
sugar
pineapple
flowers
eight

Across

2. Colorful _____ grow in Hawaii.
4. The 50th state.
6. _____ cane grows on the islands.
7. Hawaii has _____ large islands.

Down

1. The islands are_____.
3. _____ grows in Hawaii.
5. Hawaii is made up of many _____.

    FS109037 • Reading Comprehension

Valentines

February 14 is a special day of friendship and love. Valentine's Day has been a special day since long, long ago. People like to give and receive greeting cards called **valentines** on that day. Some valentines have poems and some are funny. Some are plain and others are fancy. Valentines are often red because red is the color of the heart. Red roses and hearts stand for love. Some valentines have little Cupids with wings and arrows. An old story says that Cupid shoots arrows of love into people's hearts.

Valentines

Answer each question with a sentence.

1. When is Valentine's Day?

   _____

   _____

   _____

2. What do people do on that day?

   _____

   _____

   _____

3. What do hearts and roses stand for?

   _____

   _____

   _____

4. When did Valentine's Day start?

   _____

   _____

   _____

5. Why does Cupid have arrows?

   _____

   _____

   _____

FS109037 • Reading Comprehension

A Busy Day

What a day! Max and Gina spent the day cleaning up their park. They began by picking up the trash. Then, they painted the park benches. Last, they planted new trees. What a change they made!

A Busy Day (continued)

Read each sentence. If the sentence tells about something you learned in the story, color the picture by it. Then, go back to page 10 and color the same object on that page.

Max and Gina planted trees.

Gina helped pick up trash.

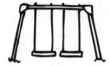

They played on the swings.

They painted the benches.

Max helped clean the park.

They planted flowers.

Max and Gina are brother and sister.

Double Trouble

My twin brothers are funny, but sometimes they make my mom crazy! Yesterday was one of those times. In the morning, they pulled all of their clothes out of their dresser. At lunch, they spilled a gallon of juice on the floor. Right after their baths, they pulled a plant out of its pot. Dirt went everywhere! Our house was a mess yesterday, but Mom says baby brothers are worth it.

FS109037 • Reading Comprehension

Double Trouble (continued)

Read each sentence. Think about the events that happened in the story. Choose the best answer and write a check mark in the box.

In the story, did the brothers . . .	Yes	No
go to school?		
take baths?		
ride bikes alone?		
plant flowers?		
make messes?		
play on a baseball team?		
spill juice?		
go on a walk?		

What can you do now that you couldn't do when you were younger? Write about it and draw a picture.

Let's Go Swimming

Michael watched his friends splashing and diving. He didn't want to be left out, but he didn't know how to swim.

Later that day, Michael asked his dad to teach him how to hold his breath underwater. They practiced all afternoon. Michael fell asleep early that night.

The next Saturday, Michael's friends met at the pool again. This time, Michael was a part of all the swimming fun. He had a good time!

FS109037 • Reading Comprehension

Let's Go Swimming (continued)

Think about Michael's feelings and how they changed throughout the story. Write a check mark to show which part of the story describes his feelings.

Michael felt...	Beginning	Middle	End
scared			
happy			
proud			
tired			
lonely			
determined			

   FS109037 • Reading Comprehension

Best Friends

Lilly and Meg had been best friends since they were both in Miss Brown's class. They spent many days planting seeds, jumping rope, and painting pictures together.

But even best friends play without each other sometimes. Lilly loved to play soccer while Meg practiced on the monkey bars. On rainy days, Lilly liked to read books, and Meg liked to count money. Some days, Lilly rushed to karate class while Meg hurried home for piano lessons. Together or alone, the girls were still best pals.

FS109037 • Reading Comprehension

Best Friends (continued)

Write two sentences to describe Lilly and two to describe Meg. In the center area, write two sentences that describe both girls.

L I L L Y

1. _____
2. _____

1. _____
2. _____

1. _____
2. _____

M E G

With which girl do you have more in common? _____

What do you have in common with her?
_____
_____

The Netherlands

In the spring, miles of tulip fields bloom in the Netherlands. Farmers grow tulips to be shipped all over the world. The people march in parades that go from town to town. They visit a park that has more than six million flowers! They sing, dance, and eat special foods. Spring is tulip time in the Netherlands.

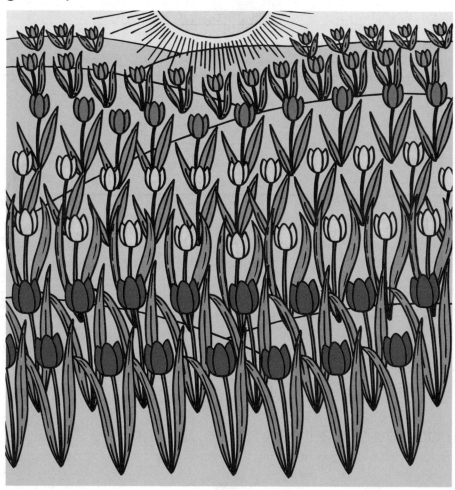

The Netherlands (continued)

Use facts from the story to fill in the puzzle. The Word Box will help you.

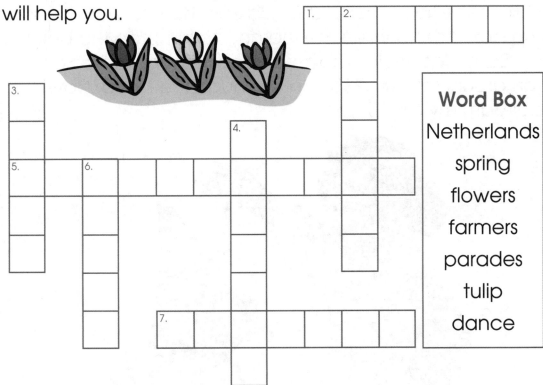

Word Box

Netherlands

spring

flowers

farmers

parades

tulip

dance

Across

1. Season when tulips grow
5. Country where tulips are grown
7. These people grow tulips.

Down

2. The people march in _____ through town.
3. The people _____ and sing.
4. Tulips are _____.
6. Spring is _____ time.

 FS109037 • Reading Comprehension

Circus Dog

I trained my dog Sam to do some tricks. First, I put a box on the floor. Then, I showed Sam how to walk around the box. After a while, he learned to jump on the box. For Sam's last trick, I made a hoop with my arms. Sam ran around me and jumped through the hoop. Now, I call Sam my circus dog!

FS109037 • Reading Comprehension

Circus Dog

Read each sentence. Write a number on each dog's tag to show the order in which things happened in the story.

I made a hoop.

I put a box on the floor.

Sam jumped on the box.

Sam jumped through the hoop.

I call Sam my circus dog.

What kind of pet would you like to train? What would your pet do?

_____
_____
_____
_____

FS109037 • Reading Comprehension

A Sweet Surprise

I remember when my brother, James, learned how to ride a bike. My mom made him a cake and iced it to look like a bicycle wheel.

I wanted a cake of my own, so I had to learn how to ride, too. The first time my mom held the back of the seat for me. I was scared! The second time, I tipped and fell into Mr. Lee's tulips! But the third time, I kept going and going!

That night after dinner, my mom set a round cake on the table. The icing was white with a black tire and spokes drawn on top. At last—my very own bicycle cake!

FS109037 • Reading Comprehension

A Sweet Surprise (continued)

The sentence on each cake tells something that happened in the story. Find the sentence on one of the bicycles that tells why it happened. Draw a line to match the pair.

It was my first try.

I landed in the neighbor's flowers.

I tipped and fell.

My mom held the seat for me.

My mom made a cake for me.

I learned to ride a bike.

My mom made a cake for James.

James learned to ride a bike.

A Deer's Antlers

This deer is called a **buck**. Bucks are the only deer that grow antlers. His antlers began to grow in the spring. They had fuzzy skin on them. The antlers inside were hard. The buck's antlers grew and grew in the summer. In the fall, the fuzzy skin came off. When winter came, the antlers fell off, too. But it didn't hurt at all. Next spring, the buck will start to grow even bigger antlers.

A Deer's Antlers (continued)

Read each sentence. Write its number on the correct deer's antlers.

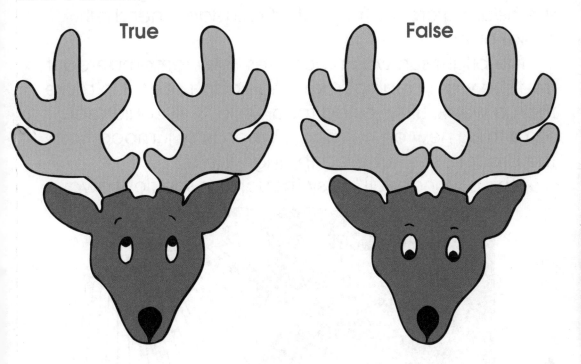

True   False

1. All deer grow antlers.
2. A deer's antlers begin to grow in the fall.
3. At first, the antlers had fuzzy skin.
4. The antlers will never grow back.
5. Antlers are soft.
6. Antlers grow back bigger each year.
7. Deer lose their antlers in winter.

FS109037 • Reading Comprehension

Bitsy's Big Day

Bitsy woke up. She could feel the warm sun on her back. She stretched her six legs. As Bitsy began to move, she heard a crack. Then, all of a sudden, her shell broke open.

The bright sun was in her eyes. Bitsy remembered the tree she was hanging from. She hadn't seen it in more than a week. Bitsy rested for a while. She could feel something new on her back. When Bitsy jumped from the branch, she fluttered through the air.

"This is wonderful!" Bitsy thought as she flew away.

Bitsy's Big Day (continued)

Write a sentence to answer each question.

1. What is Bitsy?

   _____

   _____

2. Why was today special for Bitsy?

   _____

   _____

3. Why hadn't Bitsy seen the tree for about a week?

   _____

   _____

4. What made the cracking sound?

   _____

   _____

5. Why did Bitsy feel something new on her back?

   _____

   _____

FS109037 • Reading Comprehension

Elephant Baby

Elephants are very smart, but a baby elephant has many things to learn. When a baby elephant is born, all the elephants in the family gather around. The mother uses her trunk to help her new calf stand up. At first, the baby might trip over her own trunk when she walks. Before long, she can travel with her family. They will teach her how to use her trunk to suck up water and put it in her mouth. She will learn which plants are good to eat and how to grab them with her trunk. Elephant babies roll in the mud to have fun and cool off. They blow dust on themselves to keep off bugs. They like to chase and climb on each other.

Elephant Baby (continued)

Read the title of each list. For each list, write three facts from the story.

What Elephant Babies Learn

1. _____

2. _____

3. _____

How Elephant Babies Play

1. _____

2. _____

3. _____

    FS109037 • Reading Comprehension

Buffalo Bill

Have you ever heard of Buffalo Bill? His real name was William Frederick Cody. Buffalo Bill was born in 1846. When he was fourteen years old, he became a rider for the Pony Express. He helped carry mail across the American West. Later, he worked as an army scout.

Some railroad men hired Buffalo Bill to hunt for buffalo. They needed buffalo meat to feed the workers who were laying railroad tracks through Kansas. Buffalo Bill Cody got his name for his skill at hunting buffalo.

Buffalo Bill

Use facts from the story to fill in the puzzle.
The Word Box will help you.

Word Box

buffalo
Kansas
Pony
railroad
Cody
Bill

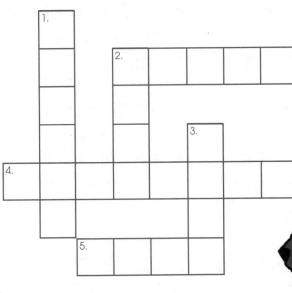

Across

2. These animals were hunted.

4. Men built a _____ through Kansas.

5. William Frederick _____ was Buffalo Bill's real name.

Down

1. The railroad workers in _____ needed food.

2. Cody became known as Buffalo _____ .

3. When he was young, Buffalo Bill worked as a _____ Express rider.

New Year's Promise

Alex awoke early. It was January 2. Today was the day that she would keep her New Year's promise. She had promised to make her bed every day before school. Alex lifted her cat Tuffy from the end of the bed. She pulled the sheets up tight and fluffed the pillows. Then, she smoothed the blanket.

Alex ran downstairs to the kitchen. "I did it! I kept my promise!" she shouted.

But the kitchen was quiet. No one was there. Then, Alex saw the morning newspaper on the counter. The paper said "Sunday" at the top. Oh no! Alex went back to bed.

New Year's Promise (continued)

Number the New Year's hats in order to retell the story.
Then, color them using the code.

1st = orange   2nd = green   3rd = red

4th = yellow   5th = purple   6th = blue

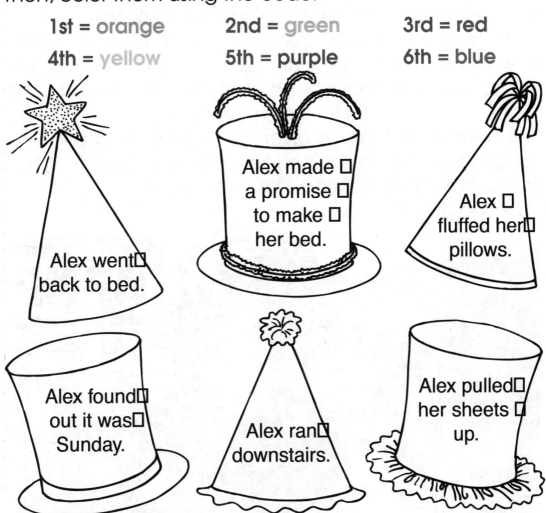

Alex went☐
back to bed.

Alex made ☐
a promise ☐
to make ☐
her bed.

Alex ☐
fluffed her☐
pillows.

Alex found☐
out it was☐
Sunday.

Alex ran☐
downstairs.

Alex pulled☐
her sheets ☐
up.

Why did Alex go back to bed after she'd already made it?

_____

_____

33   FS109037 • Reading Comprehension

The Missing Pencil

Jenna's new pencil was very special. She earned it for writing the best poem at summer camp. Jenna decided to save the pencil for special work only.

When school started, Jenna's teacher asked the class to write a story for homework. Jenna raced home to get started. She reached in her desk drawer and found ... no pencil! Jenna looked for it all afternoon.

By dinner, Jenna had given up hope of finding the pencil. She sat down at the table. Her dad asked, "Why do you have that pencil behind your ear?"

Jenna smiled.

The Missing Pencil (continued)

The sentence on each pencil tells something that happened in the story. Find the sentence that tells why it happened at the bottom of the page. Write its number on the eraser of the pencil.

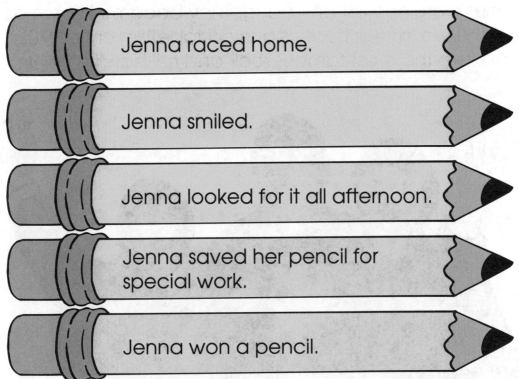

Jenna raced home.

Jenna smiled.

Jenna looked for it all afternoon.

Jenna saved her pencil for special work.

Jenna won a pencil.

1. Jenna wrote the best poem at summer camp.

2. Jenna's teacher asked her to write a story.

3. Jenna's pencil was special.

4. Jenna's pencil was missing.

5. Jenna knew where her pencil was.

The Beatles

Have you ever heard of the Beatles? They were not bugs! In the 1960s, four young lads from England played in a rock and roll band. They were John, Paul, George, and Ringo. They called themselves **The Beatles**. The Beatles were not just any band. They became known all over the world. The Beatles played together until 1970. They were the most famous rock and roll band of all time.

FS109037 • Reading Comprehension

The Beatles (continued)

Read each sentence. If it is true, write its number under the people. If it is not true, write its number under the bugs. Then, answer the question at the bottom.

1. The Beatles were from England.
2. The Beatles stopped playing together in 1960.
3. The band had six people.
4. The Beatles were only famous in England.
5. Ringo was one of the Beatles.
6. The group played rock and roll.

Who were the Beatles?

_____

_____

_____

_____

The City Mouse
and the Country Mouse

Once upon a time, the city mouse went to visit her friend in the country. The country mouse made a simple meal. Nuts, seeds, and a little dry cheese were all she had. The city mouse told the country mouse about her grand life in a big house in the city. She asked the country mouse to come for a visit. So the country mouse did. The city mouse made a meal of the fine food that was left over after a party in the big house. There were cheeses, cake crumbs, breads, and fruits. The country mouse had never eaten so well. She wished she could live in the city, too. Just then, the door opened, and in ran a cat! The two mice hurried away and hid in a dark corner. The country mouse told the city mouse, "I would rather be happy in my little home eating nuts and dry cheese than live here in fear for my life eating cake." And so she went home to the country.

The City Mouse and
the Country Mouse (continued)

Put the sentences in story order. Color the cheeses using this code:

1st = brown   **2nd = blue**   **3rd = red**

4th = yellow   **5th = green**

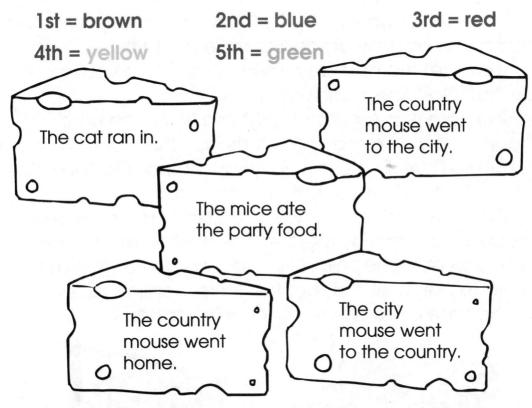

The cat ran in.

The country mouse went to the city.

The mice ate the party food.

The country mouse went home.

The city mouse went to the country.

Why was the country mouse happy to go home?

_____

_____

_____

_____

The Hare and the Turtle

One day, the hare made fun of the turtle for being so slow.

"I get where I want to go quicker than you think," said the turtle. "I'll prove it to you in a race."

The hare laughed. "That's the funniest thing I've ever heard." He eagerly agreed to race the turtle.

They met the next day. The fox said, "On your mark! Get set! Go!" The race was on.

The hare was far out of sight in a flash. The hare thought he would make the turtle see how foolish it was to race a hare. So he lay down by the path to take a nap until the turtle caught up with him.

The turtle kept going slowly, on and on. He passed the sleeping hare. By the time the hare woke up, the turtle was near the finish line. The hare ran as fast as he could to get there first, but the turtle won the race.

The race is not always won by the fastest!

The Hare and the Turtle (continued)

Think about the animals in the story. Write a check mark to show which animal is talking.

	Hare	Turtle
I am slow.		
I think I am fastest.		
I won the race.		
I laughed at others.		
I keep going and going.		
I am the wise one.		
I feel foolish now.		

Why did the hare lose the race?

_____

_____

_____

_____

Cars of the Past

In times past, most people used a horse and buggy to get around. Only a few rich people had cars. Then, Henry Ford went into the business of making cars. His cars were low in price, trustworthy, and easy to take care of.

His cars were different from cars today. To fill the gas tank, the people inside the car had to get out and then take out the seat. Sometimes the car did not start in cold weather until the driver poured hot water under the hood. Sometimes it could not get up a hill because the gas could not flow into the engine. So the driver had to roll back down the hill. Cars did not come with bumpers or mirrors as they do today. The owner had to pay extra. Still, people loved Ford's cars, and he sold millions of them.

FS109037 • Reading Comprehension

Cars of the Past (continued)

Write a sentence about how cars were
different in the past. Under it, write another
sentence that tells how that has changed.

A car of the past

Today's car

A car of the past

Today's car

Frog in Winter

Winter is coming. A little tree frog rests on a leaf in the sun. It has been hunting for food. Soon the weather will be too cold for the frog to stay warm. It will have to find cover. It may lie snugly under some dead leaves or in a hole in a tree. There, it will go into a deep sleep. The little frog will not move until spring. The frog will breathe through its skin. When the sun melts the snow and wakes up the plants, the little tree frog will wake up, too.

FS109037 • Reading Comprehension

Frog in Winter (continued)

Use facts from the story to fill in the puzzle. The Word Box will help you.

Word Box

warm

move

spring

frog

breathes

winter

leaves

Across

1. A tree frog sleeps all ____.

2. The frog does not ____.

5. The frog ____ through its skin.

6. It wakes up in the _____.

Down

1. The frog must find a place to stay _____.

3. It may sleep under dead _____.

4. A little tree _____

Beatrix Potter

Have you read a book called **The Tale of Peter Rabbit** by Beatrix Potter? When Beatrix was a little girl, she was alone much of the time. But her parents let her have some furry friends. She kept rabbits, mice, snails, and even bats. She liked to draw pictures of them. For a while, she studied art. When she was grown, Beatrix heard about a little boy who was sick. She wrote a story to cheer him up. She drew some pictures for the story, too. It was a story about rabbits. Children today still enjoy reading Beatrix's rabbit story. Can you guess what story it was?

Beatrix Potter (continued)

Read each sentence. Write a number on each rabbit to show the order in which things happened in the story.

 As a girl, Beatrix had little animals for friends.

 Children today like to read about Peter Rabbit.

 Beatrix liked to draw pictures of her animals.

 Beatrix heard about a sick boy.

 Beatrix wrote a story about rabbits.

Would you like to read **The Tale of Peter Rabbit**? Tell why or why not.

The Blue Marble

"Hey, Mark, check out my new marbles," Steven called. Mark ran over to look. Steven was showing off his favorite blue marble when his mother called him. "I'll be back," Steven said to Mark.

When Steven returned, Mark was gone and so was Steven's best blue marble. Steven turned and saw Mark walking toward him. "You took my marble, and I want it back!" Steven shouted.

"No I didn't!" yelled Mark. He ran home, angry at his friend.

Steven went inside for dinner. On the table, he spotted something blue. "My marble!" he shouted happily.

"Yes, you left it there when I called you in earlier," his mother said.

Suddenly, Steven didn't feel so happy.

The Blue Marble (continued)

The sentence on each marble tells something that happened in the story. Find the sentence that tells why it happened at the bottom of the page. Write its number in the marble.

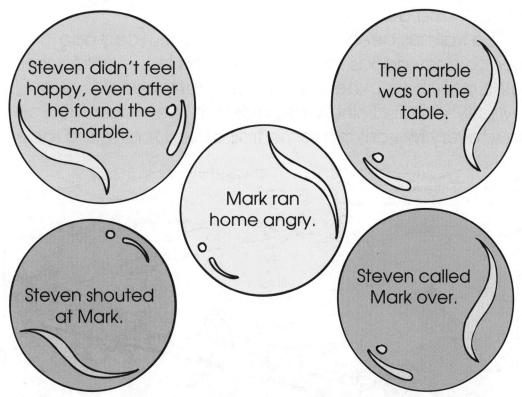

1. Steven wanted to show Mark his marbles.
2. Steven thought Mark had taken his blue marble.
3. He had not taken the marble.
4. Steven forgot it there.
5. Steven knew that Mark had not taken his marble.

FS109037 • Reading Comprehension

A Long Race

Every year, sled drivers meet in Alaska to race their teams of dogs. The race is over one thousand miles long. It lasts for more than a week. The drivers and dogs face dangers on the trail. Sometimes there are snowstorms, wild animals, and deep snow.

The trail has been there for many years. Long ago, it was used to carry goods to people working in the gold mines. Later, a terrible sickness broke out. Many people were saved when medicine was carried to them over the trail. Now, every March, the same trail is used for the big race.

A Long Race (continued)

Read each sentence. Color the sled **red** if it is true. Color the sled **blue** if it is not true.

Sometimes there are dangers in the race.

The race lasts for a day and a half.

The trail was built for the railroad.

The big race is in June.

Long ago, the trail led to gold mines.

The race covers more than a thousand miles.

FS109037 • Reading Comprehension

School Days

"Rosie, it's time to get up. You don't want to be late for school again today," Mom called.

Rosie threw on her clothes. She ran to the kitchen and reached for a warm pancake. After quickly eating her food, Rosie grabbed her backpack and ran for the door. "I love you, Mom!" she called as she rushed to the bus stop.

The clock radio came on. Tony got dressed and went down to the kitchen. He poured a bowl of cornflakes and read the back of the box as he ate. Tony put his dishes in the sink and found his backpack waiting by the door. "I'm ready," he called as his mom came in.

"Great. We have plenty of time to walk you to school," his mom said.

School Days (continued)

Think about the children in the stories. Write a checkmark to show who is being described.

	Rosie	Tony
Awakened by mother		
Going to school today		
Ate breakfast		
Rode the bus		
Walked to school		
Seemed to be rushed		
Seemed to have time		

Who is more likely to have forgotten something at home? Why?

_____

Page 3

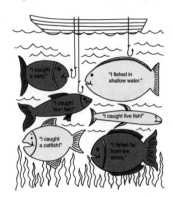

Page 5

Sentences may be in any order: Whales sleep close to the top of the water. Whales float. Part of its brain stays awake. They come to the surface to breathe.
Answers will vary.

Page 7

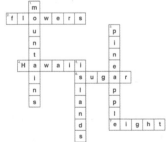

Page 9

1. Valentine's Day is February 14.
2. They give and receive valentines.
3. They stand for love.
4. Valentine's Day started long ago.
5. He shoots love into people's hearts.

Page 11

Child should not color the swings, the flowers, or the brother and sister. The rest of the picture should be colored.

Page 13

In the story, did the brothers . . .	Yes	No
go to school?		✓
take baths?	✓	
ride bikes alone?		✓
plant flowers?		✓
make messes?	✓	
play on a baseball team?		✓
spill juice?	✓	
go on a walk?		✓

Page 15

Michael felt...	Beginning	Middle	End
scared	✓		
happy			✓
proud			✓
tired		✓	
lonely	✓		
determined		✓	

Page 17

Lilly played soccer,
Lilly read books, or
Lilly took karate class.

Lilly and Meg planted seeds,
Lilly and Meg jumped rope, or
Lilly and Meg painted pictures.

Meg liked the monkey bars,
Meg counted money, or
Meg took piano lessons.
Bottom answers will vary.

Page 19

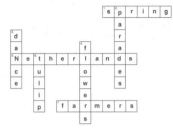

Page 21

3, 2, 5, 1, 4

Page 23

Page 25

True: 3, 6, 7
False: 1, 2, 4, 5

Page 27

Answers will vary.
1. Bitsy is a butterfly.
2. She came out of her shell and flew as a butterfly.
3. Bitsy had been inside her shell.
4. Bitsy's shell made the cracking sound when it split open.
5. She had grown wings.

         FS109037 • Reading Comprehension

Page 29
What Baby Elephants Learn
1. to stand up
2. to walk
3. to suck up water

How Elephant Babies Play
1. roll in the mud
2. chase each other
3. climb on each other

Page 31
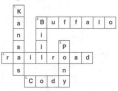

Page 33

She discovered that it was Sunday, not a school day.

Page 35
2, 5, 4, 3, 1

Page 37
Beatles: 1, 5, 6
Bugs: 2, 3, 4
The Beatles were a famous rock and roll band from England.

Page 39

She felt safer at home.

Page 41

	Hare	Turtle
I am slow.		✓
I think I am fastest.	✓	
I won the race.		✓
I laughed at others.	✓	
I keep going and going.		✓
I am the wise one.		✓
I feel foolish now.	✓	

Page 43
Answers will vary.

Page 45
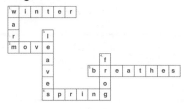

Page 47
1, 5, 2, 3, 4
Answers will vary.

Page 49
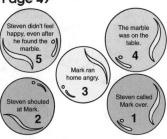

Page 51

Page 53

	Rosie	Tony
Awakened by mother	✓	
Going to school today	✓	✓
Ate breakfast	✓	✓
Rode the bus	✓	
Walked to school		✓
Seemed to be rushed	✓	
Seemed to have time		✓

Rosie may have forgotten something because she is in a hurry.

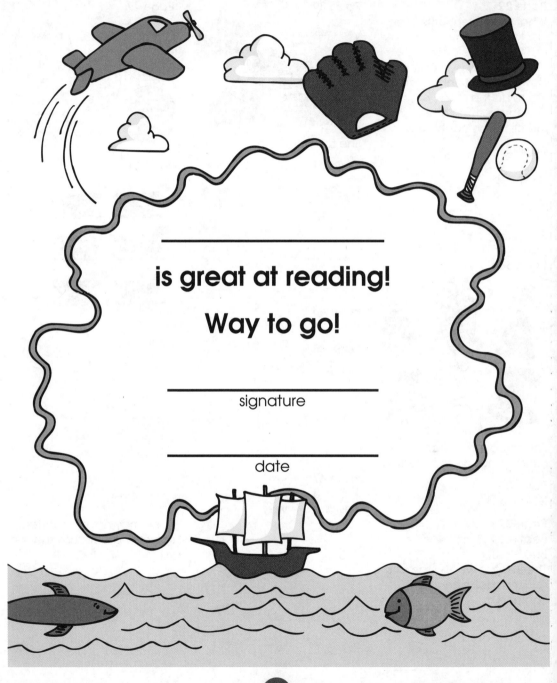

_____

is great at reading!
Way to go!

_____
signature

_____
date

FS109037 • Reading Comprehension